OUR DAILY BREAD® FOR Preschoolers

Written by Crystal Bowman & Teri McKinley

Illustrated by Luke Flowers

90 BIG MOMENTS WITH GOD

Our Daily Bread
Publishing™

To Andrew Hulst and Timothy Lee—
you are proof of God's amazing power and love.

C.B. and T.M.

For my grandfather and hero, Grandpa Benno.
A shining example of God's unwavering love every day of your life.

L.F.

Our Daily Bread for Preschoolers
© 2016 by Crystal Bowman and Teri McKinley
Illustrations by Luke Flowers and © 2016 by Discovery House (Our Daily Bread Publishing)
All rights reserved.

Requests for permission to quote from this book should be directed to:
Permissions Department, Our Daily Bread Publishing, P.O. Box 3566, Grand Rapids, MI 49501,
or contact us by e-mail at permissionsdept@odb.org.

Design by Kris Nelson/StoryLook Design

Library of Congress Cataloging-in-Publication Data
Names: Bowman, Crystal, author. | Flowers, Luke, illustrator.
Title: Our daily bread for preschoolers : 90 big moments with God / written
    by Crystal Bowman & Teri McKinley ; illustrated by Luke Flowers.
Description: Grand Rapids : Discovery House, 2016.
Identifiers: LCCN 2015049198 | ISBN 9781627074759
Subjects: LCSH: Children--Prayers and devotions.
Classification: LCC BV4870 .B643 2016 | DDC 249--dc23
LC record available at http://lccn.loc.gov/2015049198
2014037748

Printed in China
20 21 22 23 24 25 26 / 8 7 6 5 4 3 2

Introduction

Young children are curious and eager to learn. They love exploring God's amazing creation and wonder how everything came to be. During the preschool years, parents have a unique opportunity to teach children about God and His revelation to us through the Bible.

The devotions in *Our Daily Bread for Preschoolers* are designed to help you make the most of these important years. Many of the daily readings teach children about characters from the Bible and the stories that surround them. Other readings point a child to God and how to know Him as their creator and friend.

Through the daily readings, children will learn that God made the world, and that He sustains and cares for His created things. They will learn that God speaks to them through the Bible, and they can speak to God through their prayers. Some of the readings remind children of God's gifts and blessings, and some of them focus on Jesus—God's greatest gift of all.

Each daily reading includes a short Bible verse, a devotion, and a prayer. A simple question is also included on each page to engage children and encourage a response. As you read this book to your children, you can help them understand that they are precious to God, that He is always with them, and that He loves them very much.

—Crystal and Teri

The Best Book of All

Do you like to look at books? Do you like to hear the words read to you? Some books tell stories. Some books teach you things you should know. There are many good books to read, but the Bible is the best book of all! The Bible tells how God made the world and the animals and people.

The Bible tells us that God is great. It tells how we can please God and get to know Him. The Bible has stories about people who lived a long time ago. And it has lots of stories about Jesus, who is God's very own Son. This book is not the Bible. But this book will help you learn about the Bible and how much God loves you. —C.B.

What book is the girl in the picture reading?

PRAYER

Dear God, the Bible comes from You. I know Your words are always true.

Who Wrote the Bible?

Every book was written by someone. A person who writes a book is called an *author*. Many times, an author's name is on the front of a book. But the Bible doesn't have an author's name on the cover. That's because the Bible is a very special book. Do you know who wrote the Bible?

A long time ago, many people wrote down the words in the Bible. But they aren't the real authors of the Bible. God is! God told all of those people what to write. Because of His love for us, God told us important things. If you want to learn those things, all you have to do is open your Bible and read. —T.M.

Whose words are in the Bible?

PRAYER

Thank You, God, for the words You share to show us just how much You care.

Then God looked over all he had made,
and he saw that it was very good!

GENESIS 1:31 NLT

God's Beautiful World

The very first page of the Bible tells how God made a big, beautiful world. He made the sky and the land. He made lakes and oceans and rivers. He made fish to swim in the water and birds to fly in the air. He made plants and trees and pretty flowers. He made tiny ants that crawl on the ground and giant elephants that live in the jungle. Everything God made was very good. What do you see when you go for a walk or look out your window? Do you see trees and flowers? Do you see birds and bugs? Maybe you can see a mountain or a lake. God made all those things, and He made them for you to enjoy! —C.B.

What sound does a bird make?

PRAYER

**Thank You, Lord, for all I see.
You made the pretty world for me!**

He calls out to the earth from the sunrise
in the east to the sunset in the west.

PSALM 50:1 NIRV

God's Big Sun

Have you seen the big sun in the sky? How do you think it got there? When God made our world, He also made the sun and put it way up high in the sky. God made the sun to shine during the day to give us light so we can see. He made the sun to warm the earth. God

made the sun to help plants and trees and
flowers grow. Every day the sun comes up in
the morning to give us the light and warmth
we need. When you see the sun, you can say
"thank You" to God for putting it in the sky.
—C.B.

What color
is the daytime sun?

**Lord, You made the great big sun
to shine its light on everyone.**

God Makes People

God wanted to share His big, beautiful world with someone special. So God made a man named Adam and a woman named Eve. Adam and Eve were different from all the other things God made. They could talk to God and He could talk to them. God wanted Adam and Eve to enjoy the fruit from the trees He made. He wanted them to walk by the river and see the pretty flowers. God made Adam and Eve to be like Him. Everything God made was special, but Adam and Eve were the most special of all.

Did you know you are special too? God made you so you can talk to Him. He made you to enjoy all the things He made! —C.B.

How are people different from animals?

**Lord, You made me special too.
I'm glad that I can talk to You.**

The birds in the sky build nests by the waters.
They sing among the branches.

PSALM 104:12 NIRV

Happy Birds

Sometimes on a bright sunny day you can
hear birds tweeting. They sit way up high
on tree branches. They fly around to look at
God's beautiful world. As they look down
they sing happy songs that bring music to the
earth. The birds are happy because God takes
care of them. He gives them food to eat. He

watches over them all day long. Do you know that God watches over you too? God gives you food to eat and takes care of you every day. Just like the birds, you can sing a happy song. You can thank God for His love. —T.M.

How many birds
can you count?

PRAYER

**I can sing a happy song
because You're with me all day long.**

Time to Rest

Do you know what God did after He made
the world? He rested. In six days, God made
everything we see. Then on the seventh day
He did no work at all. God doesn't get tired
like we do. But He wanted to show us that it's
good to rest. It's fun to run and swing outside.
It's fun to play with your toys and games in

the house. But when you get tired, it's good to rest. You can take a nap in the afternoon. And God made the nighttime so we can sleep. Resting is good for you. After you rest you feel better. After you rest you have more energy, so you can play again. It's good to play, and it's good to rest. —C.B.

What is the child doing in the picture?

PRAYER

Thank You, Lord, You know what's best— my growing body needs to rest.

The earth belongs to the LORD.
And so does everything in it.

PSALM 24:1 NIRV

God Owns It All

God owns everything in the whole world. That's because He made it all! The plants and animals, the trees and rocks, the clouds and sun—they all belong to God. God owns the rain and lightning, the snow and mountains, the oceans and sand. He owns the green grass and tiny ants that crawl in the grass. Even the things you have belong to God, who lets you use them. Since God owns everything, He's in charge. He knows the best way to take care of things because He made them. We can trust Him to take care of our things—and of us! —T.M.

Who owns the moon?

PRAYER

**The snow and sun, the ants that crawl,
the rocks and trees—You own them all.**

So the LORD God sent the man
out of the Garden of Eden.

GENESIS 3:23 GW

A Sad Day

God loved Adam and Eve very much. He
wanted them to obey Him. The garden where
they lived had many trees with good fruit to
eat. God told Adam and Eve they could eat
from every tree except for one. But one day,
Adam and Eve disobeyed. They ate the fruit
they were not supposed to eat. God was
sad when they disobeyed Him. Adam and

Eve were sad too. They had to leave their beautiful garden. But God still loved them.

God wants us to obey Him because He knows what is best for us. When we disobey God it is called sin. Everybody sins—even people who love God. But when we sin we can tell God we are sorry. He will forgive us because He loves us. —C.B.

Why do Adam and Eve look sad?

Dear God, please help me every day:
help me to listen and obey.

My child, pay attention to my words.
Listen closely to what I say.

PROVERBS 4:20 ICB

Stop and Look

Have you ever seen a stop sign? If you're riding in a car and you come to a stop sign, it's important for the driver to stop. It's important to look both ways to make sure another car is not coming. Stop signs help to keep drivers safe so they don't crash into each other.

God's words in the Bible can help to keep us safe. God loves us and wants to take care of us, so He tells us how He wants us to live. Sometimes you might want to do something that you know is wrong. Before you do that, stop and look. Ask God to help you do the right thing. When you do the right thing, God is pleased. —C.B.

What color is a stop sign?

PRAYER

**Help me, Lord, to do what's right.
Help me please You day and night.**

Noah's Big Boat

One day God looked down from heaven. He
was sad because the people He made were
being bad. They did not love God or obey
Him. They did things God told them not to
do. God decided to send a flood to make the
bad people go away. But God saw that Noah
loved Him. So God wanted to save Noah and
his family. He told Noah to build a big boat

called an *ark*. God told Noah how long and tall to make the boat. He told Noah what kind of wood to use. God told Noah to bring two of every kind of animal onto the boat. Noah did just what God told him to do.

When the flood came, God took care of Noah and his family. And do you know what? God still takes care of people who love Him.
—T.M.

What animals can
you name on the ark?

PRAYER

**Even though I'm still a kid,
help me love You like Noah did.**

> "I will put my rainbow in the clouds
> to be a sign of my promise to the earth."
>
> GENESIS 9:13 GW

God's Promise

Have you ever seen a big, bright rainbow
in the sky? When the weather is just right,
beautiful colors appear. Rainbows are very
special because they remind us of a promise
God made. After the flood, Noah and his
family came out of the ark. Noah thanked
God by giving Him a special gift called an

offering. The offering made God happy, and He made a promise to Noah. God said He would never send a big flood to cover the world again. Then He put a rainbow in the sky as a sign of His promise. The next time you see a rainbow, you can remember God's promise too. —T.M.

How many colors can you name in the rainbow?

PRAYER

Thank You, God, for rainbows high that show Your promise in the sky.

God Makes the Rain

God promised He would never flood the whole earth again. But we still need rain! When you see big dark clouds, it can mean that rain is coming. As puffy storm clouds move across the sky, raindrops fall all the way to the ground. The thirsty land drinks up the rain. The rain helps the plants grow. God planned it that way! God knows that the earth needs rain. He knows that the grass and flowers and trees need special care. He knows because He created everything. God makes the clouds and the rain. He makes the plants and helps them grow. When you see raindrops you can remember that God takes care of His creation. —T.M.

What is coming out of the clouds?

PRAYER

**Lord, You make the tall grass grow.
You send rain to the ground below.**

> "I will make you into a great nation, and I will bless you."
>
> GENESIS 12:2 NIV

Abram Moves Away

Abram was a man who lived a long time ago. One day God told Abram, "I want you to move to another country." Abram loved God, so he did what God told him to do. Abram took his wife, Sarai, with him. God led them to a new place. One night God gave Abram a special promise. God told Abram to look into the sky. "Look at the stars, Abram," God said. "Can you count them? That's how many people will be in your family someday. I will give this land to them, and your family will become a big nation." Abram loved God. He knew God's promise would come true. —C.B.

Why did Abram move away?

PRAYER

You bless us when we follow You and do the things You ask us to.

Millions of Stars

The sky is very dark at night. But if you look up high, you can see lots of tiny, twinkling stars. God told Abram to count the stars. Do you think you can count them? No way! There are too many stars for anyone to count. God made millions and millions of stars and put them in the sky to shine at night. There are so many stars we can't even see them all! Even though we cannot count them, God can. He counts every one and He gives each star a name.

The next time you look at the stars, remember how great God is. He knows every star in the sky. And He knows you too! —C.B.

How many stars can you count in the picture?

PRAYER

Lord, You count the stars up high that twinkle in the big dark sky.

A Baby Boy

When Abram was very old, God changed
his name. Abram was now "Abraham." And
God changed Sarai's name to "Sarah." God
promised again that Abraham's family would
be very big. God told them that He would
give them a son. Abraham thought he and
Sarah were too old to have children. But do

you know what? God gave them a baby boy!
They named him Isaac. After many years they
had grandchildren and great-grandchildren,
just like God had promised.

God gives us lots of promises in the Bible.
He kept His promise to Abraham and Sarah.
And He will keep all of His promises to you.
—C.B.

What did Abraham and Sarah name their baby boy?

PRAYER

**Lord, nothing is too hard for You.
Your promises are always true.**

Filled with Joy

God did a great thing by giving Abraham and
Sarah a baby when they were old. The Bible
has many stories of other great things God
did. There is even a song in the Bible about
some of the great things God did for His
people. It says the people were filled with joy
because of the great things God did for them.

God does great things for you too! He gives you clothes to wear and food to eat. He listens to you when you pray. He gives you friends and family who love you. He helps you learn new things. When you think about the great things God does for you, doesn't that make you happy? You can say "thank You" to God for what He has done. —T.M.

What is one thing God has done for you?

PRAYER

Lord, You are great in many ways. I'm filled with joy and give You praise.

Rebekah became his wife that day. Isaac loved her very much. So he was comforted after his mother's death.

GENESIS 24:67 ERV

A Wife for Isaac

Isaac was sad when his mother died. It was time for him to get married, and his father, Abraham, wanted Isaac to marry the right girl. He sent his servant to find a wife for Isaac. The man prayed near a well. He said, "Dear God, may the right girl give water to me and my camels." Before the prayer was over, a girl named Rebekah came near. She gave the servant and his camels water to drink. The servant knew this was the wife God wanted for Isaac. Rebekah left her family and went to Isaac's home. Isaac loved Rebekah and she helped him feel better.

The story of Isaac and Rebekah shows that God cares about us. He helps us when we are sad. And He listens to people who pray.
—T.M.

How many camels can you count?

PRAYER

God, I know You always care.
Thank You that You hear my prayer.

A Big Hug

What makes you feel sad? You might be sad if you are sick and can't play outside. You might be sad if you break your favorite toy. And you might be sad if your grandma lives far away and you can't see her for a while. It's okay to be sad sometimes. But when you think about how much God loves you, you can feel happy again. When you are sad and someone gives you a big hug, you feel better. That's how God wants you to feel.

The next time you are sad, just remember how much God loves you. You can give yourself a big hug and feel good inside! —C.B.

Who do you like to hug?

PRAYER

**Thank You, Lord, that when I'm sad
Your love for me will make me glad.**

Jacob and Esau

Isaac loved his wife, Rebekah, very much. She wanted to have a child, so Isaac prayed for her. He asked God to give her a baby. God heard Isaac's prayer. But He didn't give them one baby—He gave them two! Rebekah had twin boys named Jacob and Esau. Do you remember how God promised to give Abraham a great big family? Jacob and Esau were Abraham's grandsons.

When Jacob grew up, he had twelve sons. They were Abraham's great-grandsons. Abraham's family was getting bigger and bigger just like God said it would! God blessed Abraham's family. You can ask God to bless your family too. —C.B.

How many people
are in your family?

PRAYER

Lord, please bless my family too.
Keep us safe in all we do.

Be Kind

God loves us and He wants us to be loving and kind to our friends and family. But sometimes brothers and sisters fight over a toy. Sometimes friends say mean things. That's not how we should treat others. There are many ways you can be kind. You can share your crayons with someone who wants to color a picture. You can share your cookie with someone who wants a bite. And you can be kind by the words you say. Do you say "please" and "thank you"? Do you say "I'm sorry"? When you say those words, you are being kind. Being kind makes other people happy. It makes God happy too! —C.B.

How is the boy in the picture being kind to his friend?

PRAYER

Lord, help me to be kind today in what I do and what I say.

Joseph Forgives His Brothers

Joseph was one of Jacob's sons. He had ten older brothers. One day his brothers were mean and sent him away. Joseph went to Egypt where his life was hard. He even went to jail when he didn't do anything wrong. But God was with Joseph. Soon, Joseph was in charge of everything!

Many years later, Joseph's brothers came to Egypt to buy food. When Joseph saw them, he knew they were his brothers. But when they saw Joseph, they didn't know he was their little brother. When they found out, they were scared. "Joseph will use his power to get back at us," they said. But Joseph chose to forgive his brothers. "God sent me to Egypt to help you," he told them.

When people are mean, you can be nice anyway. You can forgive them like Joseph did. When you forgive, you show God's love. —T.M.

Who can you be nice to today?

PRAYER

Help me forgive my family and friends, and show them Your love that never ends.

"You will come and pray to me. And I will listen to you."

JEREMIAH 29:12 NIRV

God Listens

Sometimes grown-ups are busy. When kids talk, grown-ups don't always listen. It can be hard when you have something to say but no one will listen to you. It's never like that with God. He listens to you every time you pray. If you pray in the morning, God will listen. If you pray in the afternoon or at night, God will listen. You can tell Him anything you want to say. He is never too busy to listen to you! God listened to Abraham and Isaac when they prayed to Him. He will listen to your prayers too. God likes to hear your prayers. He is a good listener! —C.B.

What do you want to tell God?

PRAYER

**Lord, You listen when I pray.
I know You hear the words I say.**

When the child was old enough, she brought him to
Pharaoh's daughter, and he became her son.
Pharaoh's daughter named him Moses.

EXODUS 2:10 GW

A Baby in a Basket

There was a new king in Egypt. He was afraid
God's people would take over his kingdom.
He made a bad rule that all baby boys had to
be thrown into the Nile River.

One baby boy wasn't thrown into the
river. His mother secretly put him in a basket
instead. But the king's daughter found the

basket! She opened the basket and saw the baby crying. She made the boy her son and named him Moses.

God had a special plan for Moses. Even the king couldn't stop it. God has special plans for you too. You can pray and ask God to help you know His plans. —T.M.

What color is the basket
in the picture?

You Are Precious to God

Do you know what the word *precious* means? It means something costs a lot of money or is loved very much. Fancy stones like diamonds are called "precious stones" because they are worth so much.

In the Bible, King David thanked God for thinking precious thoughts about him. David knew that God's thoughts about him were worth more than money or fancy stones.

God thinks precious thoughts about you too. Even if you tried, you couldn't count all His thoughts about you! You are precious to God because He loves you. —T.M.

What colors are the precious stones in the picture?

PRAYER

Your precious thoughts help me to see how much You love and care for me.

Moses and the Burning Bush

When Moses grew up he left Egypt and lived in the desert. One day he was taking care of sheep, and he saw a bush on fire. But it was not burning up! Moses looked closely at the bush. And then he heard God call his name. Moses answered, "Here I am." God said He had an important job for Moses. The

Egyptians were being mean to God's people. God wanted Moses to go back to Egypt and save them. Moses was scared at first, but God promised to be with him. Moses obeyed God and went to Egypt.

Did you know God speaks to you too? You probably won't hear His voice in a bush. But God speaks to you through the Bible. You can learn all about God and what He wants you to know when you read His book. —T.M.

Can you read a story in the Bible with someone today?

PRAYER

**The Bible is how You talk to me.
Help me to listen carefully.**

I can do all things through Christ
because he gives me strength.

PHILIPPIANS 4:13 ICB

Be Strong

Some people have big muscles and strong
bodies. But did you know people can be
strong on the inside too? When you are
strong on the inside it means you can do the
things God wants you to do. God gave Moses
a big job. Moses didn't think he could do it,
but God helped him. God helps us do the
things He wants us to do.

When it's time to pick up your toys, God will help you be strong so you can do it. When it's time to sit still at the dinner table, God will help you be strong so you can do it. When you need to do something, just ask God to help you. Then you can be strong on the inside. —C.B.

How can you be strong today?

PRAYER

**Help me, Lord, and make me strong
to put my toys where they belong.**

Crossing the Red Sea

Moses led God's people out of Egypt. They
camped by the Red Sea. The king of Egypt
was mad and chased God's people with his
army. They were scared because they were
trapped! But God had a plan. God told

Moses, "Raise your hand over the sea." The water split apart and the people walked across on dry ground! When the Egyptians followed them, Moses raised his hand again. God made the water flow together. The army of Egypt was trapped in the water.

Sometimes God shows His power in big ways like He did for Moses. Other times God shows His power in smaller ways. Sometimes God heals people when they are sick. Sometimes God gives us what we need right when we need it. God can do anything! —T.M.

What did God tell Moses to do at the Red Sea?

PRAYER

Dear Lord, You do things big and small. You show Your power through them all.

Sing to God

How do you show people that you are happy?
Do you tell them? Do you smile or laugh?
What about singing? A song is a fun way to
show people you are happy!

Did you know the Bible tells us to sing
to God? Singing to God shows Him we are
happy because of all that He does for us.
When we sing to God we tell Him that we

love Him and that we are thinking about Him. Singing to God shows that He is important. God loves to hear you sing, no matter what you sound like.

The next time you feel happy, you can let God know with a song. Your singing is music to His ears! —T.M.

What is your favorite song to sing?

Dear Lord, I'll raise my voice and sing, for all the happiness You bring.

LORD, there is no one like you. You are great!

JEREMIAH 10:6 ERV

God Is Great

The Bible tells about many great things God did a long time ago. Can you remember some of them? God made the whole world and everything in it. He put a colorful rainbow in the sky. And He helped Moses lead many people across a big sea. Those are great things!

And God still does great things today. Only God can make it rain. Only God can make trees grow big and tall. And God is the only one who can make the stars come out at night. No one is greater than God, and nothing is greater than God's love for you. The next time you pray, you can tell God how great He is! —C.B.

Who makes the sun shine?

PRAYER

Dear God, You are the greatest one. You made the moon and stars and sun.

The LORD said to Moses, "I'm going to send you food from heaven like rain. Each day the people should go out and gather only what they need for that day."

EXODUS 16:4 GW

Bread from Heaven

God's people were hungry as they walked through the desert. God told Moses, "I will send bread from heaven for you each day." But He had rules for the bread He sent. "The people should go out and gather only what they need for that day," He told Moses. God showed His people that He would give them what they needed one day at a time. God

64

wanted the people to know they could trust Him.

Every morning, the people found bread on the ground like dew. They called the bread manna. There was plenty to eat! But if they tried to save it for the next day, it smelled bad and had worms inside. The next day, new bread would come and the people could fill their bellies again.

God knows exactly what you need too. He gives you enough for each day. God will take care of you day by day. —T.M.

What kind of food do you eat in the morning?

PRAYER

**You sent the manna from above
to show Your power and Your love.**

God Gives Us Food

Does your family buy food at a grocery store? Maybe you grow tomatoes or beans right in your own backyard. No matter where you get your food, it all comes from God. God made the animals that give us milk and eggs. God made the trees that give us apples, oranges, and mangos. God sends the rain and sunshine to help seeds sprout into wheat and corn.

In the Bible, Jesus prayed "The Lord's Prayer." In that prayer, He said, "Give us today our daily bread." By saying those words, Jesus taught us how to pray. Just like Jesus, we can ask God to give us food every day. And before you eat the food He gives you, remember to say, "Thank You!" —C.B.

Where does milk come from?

PRAYER

**Thank You, God, for food to eat,
for cheese and beans and fruit that's sweet.**

Like newborn babies, you should long
for the pure milk of God's word.

1 PETER 2:2 NIRV

Brain Food

Do you know why you need to eat food
every day? Food keeps your body strong and
healthy. Without food, you wouldn't grow.
Just like you fill your body with good food,
you need to fill your mind with good things.
Filling your mind with good things helps your
brain learn and grow. The best thing you can
fill your mind with is God's Word.

In God's Word we read stories about how much God loves His people. These stories help us learn all about God. The Bible also tells us what Jesus said while He was on earth. When we read about God's love and the words Jesus spoke, we are putting the best food into our minds. —T.M.

What do you like to eat when you are hungry?

PRAYER

Lord, help my mind to learn and grow.
Teach me what I need to know.

"I am the Lord your God. I brought you out
of the land of Egypt where you were slaves."

EXODUS 20:2 ICB

The Ten Commandments

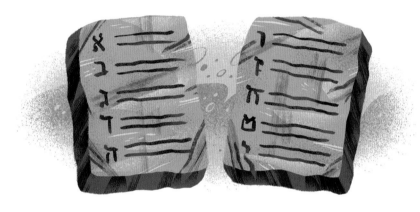

God did a great thing when He led His people
through the Red Sea. Then Moses led the
people into the desert. God would talk to
Moses so Moses could tell the people what
to do. God wanted the people to remember
that He was their God. He wanted the
people to know He loved them and cared
for them. One day God told Moses to write

down some rules. They are called the Ten Commandments. If the people followed the Ten Commandments, they would show their love for God. And they would learn how to love each other.

God loves us and cares for us too. That is why He gives us rules. God's rules keep us safe. And best of all, they show us how to love God. —C.B.

How fast can you count to 10?

PRAYER

**Lord, may I love with all my heart.
Obeying You is where I'll start.**

"Honor your father and your mother."

EXODUS 20:12 ICB

Honor Your Parents

God gave His people ten commandments. One of them says, "Honor your father and mother." The word *honor* means to listen and obey. God gave this commandment to all children. He wants them to listen to grown-ups who love them and take care of them. Maybe you live with your grandma and grandpa. Or maybe you live with an aunt or uncle. They are just like parents that God has given to you. Your parents might tell you to wash your hands or eat your vegetables. Your grandma might say it's time to go to bed. Those are important things to do! When you obey, it shows God that you honor them.

—C.B.

How can you honor
your parents today?

PRAYER

Thank You for grown-ups who care for me.
Help me to honor them happily.

> "In the future your children will ask you, 'What do these rocks mean?' Tell them the Lord stopped the water from flowing in the Jordan."

JOSHUA 4:6–7 ICB

Twelve Special Stones

God chose Joshua to lead His people into the land He had promised to give them. But first they had to cross the Jordan River. Do you know how they did it? God made the river stop flowing so His people could walk across! God told Joshua, "Ask twelve men to stop as they cross the river and pick up stones. Have them put the stones down where you stay tonight." The rocks would help the people remember the great things God did. When the people and their children saw the twelve special stones, they remembered how God helped them cross the river.

God wants us to remember the good things He does too. That's one reason God gave us the Bible. It has many stories that remind us of His love and all the good things He has done. —T.M.

How many stones can you count in the picture?

PRAYER

Thank You for stories from the past, that show Your love will always last.

*"I am the LORD your God.
I will be with you everywhere you go."*

JOSHUA 1:9 NIRV

God Is with You

Do you ever go to the park or the zoo? Do you like to ride your bike or go down the slide at the playground? Sometimes it's nice to stay home and read books or play with toys. No matter where you go or what you do, God is always with you. In the Bible, God told His people that He would be with them wherever they went. If they were living in the desert or crossing a river, He was always with them. And God is with you too!

Do you ever go to a friend's house? Do you go to school or church? Wherever you go, whether it's daytime or nighttime, God is with you. Even though you can't see Him, He is there. —C.B.

Where do you like to go?

PRAYER

**If I'm at home or far away,
You are with me every day.**

Big Walls Fall Down

When God's people crossed the Jordan River,
they came to a city called Jericho. God told
them the city was theirs. But great big walls
around the city kept them out.

So God told the people to march around the city one time each day for six days. On the seventh day they had to march around it again—seven times! The people did what God told them to do. Then they blew their trumpets and the big walls came crashing down!

God showed the people that He would always help them. He reminded them that He could do great things. The people might have thought God's plan was strange, but His plans are always right. That's because God is great!
—C.B.

What color is the wall in the picture?

PRAYER

God, You made those walls fall down. You made them tumble to the ground.

> "I am the LORD who rules over all. . . . I am the first and the last. I am the one and only God."
>
> ISAIAH 44:6 NIRV

One True God

Did you know that some people have more than one grandma? Some people have more than one brother or sister. Lots of people have many cousins. But do you know what we have only one of? We have only one true God.

There is only one God who could make the big blue ocean. There is only one God who could build giant mountains. There is only one God who could put all the stars in the sky. There is only one God who can hear the prayers of all His people. And there is only one God who loves you and calls you His child.

You can thank God for being the only One who can do all these things. —T.M.

How many grandparents do you have?

PRAYER

**There's only one God for me to love.
You made the earth and the sky above.**

A Good Friend

The Bible tells the story of a woman named
Naomi. She was sad because most of her
family had died. And life was hard because
there was no food where she lived.

A young woman named Ruth had
married Naomi's son. Now that her son was
dead, Naomi told Ruth to go back to her own
home. But Ruth would not leave Naomi. She

said, "Where you go, I'll go. And where you stay, I'll stay." So Ruth stayed with Naomi and God took care of them.

Ruth was a good friend. She helped Naomi when she was all alone. You can be a good friend like Ruth. You can help people too! —T.M.

Who can you be a good friend to today?

PRAYER

Help me to be a good friend too, by showing others love from You.

When others are happy, you should be happy with them.

ROMANS 12:15 ERV

Be Happy

What makes you happy? Lots of things can make us happy. You can be happy when it's a sunny day. You can be happy when you learn a new song. And you can be happy when it's your birthday.

There are other times when you can be happy. The Bible tells us to be happy when someone else is happy. It's one of the ways we can show God's love to others. So you can be happy with your neighbors when they get a new pet. You can be happy with your friends when it's their birthday. If you have brothers or sisters, you can be happy when they get a new game or toy.

With all those reasons to be happy, you can praise God with a big smile on your face!
—C.B.

How do you know the girls in the picture are happy?

PRAYER

**Thank You, God, for happy days.
I will give You lots of praise.**

Do not be interested only in your own life,
but be interested in the lives of others.

PHILIPPIANS 2:4 ICB

Be a Helper

Do you ever help around the house? Maybe
you pick up your dirty clothes so they can be
washed. Maybe you help set the table. Or
maybe you pick up your toys when you are
done playing. There are many things you can
do to be a helper. And do you know what?

You can help people outside your house too. If your friend falls down on the playground, you can help him up. If you have a neighbor who is older, you can bring her a snack or pick up her mail.

You can do many things, every day, to be a helper. When we help others, it's like sharing God's love with them. —T.M.

How can you be a helper today?

PRAYER

Dear God, I want to help and give, and show Your love in how I live.

> "I prayed for this child, and the LORD answered my prayer. He gave me this child."
>
> 1 SAMUEL 1:27 ERV

Baby Samuel

A woman named Hannah was sad. She wanted children but she didn't have any. Every day she prayed and asked God to give her a child. One day she said to God, "If You give me a son, I will give him back to You."

God answered Hannah's prayer and gave her a baby boy! She named him Samuel. When he was older, Hannah brought Samuel to live in God's temple. The boy could learn how to serve God there. Samuel loved God and always wanted to please Him.

Hannah knew that only God was able to answer her prayer. She said, "The Lord has filled my heart with joy. There is no one holy like the Lord." You can pray to God just like Hannah did. He is the only one who can answer your prayer. —C.B.

Why is Hannah smiling?

PRAYER

You are my God who listens and cares. You are the God who hears my prayers.

Praise the LORD. Give thanks to the LORD, because he is good.

PSALM 106:1 NIRV

Thank You, God!

Do you say "thank you" to your mom when she makes you a snack? Do you say "thank you" to your teacher when she helps you tie your shoe? Just like we say "thank you" to other people, we can tell God "thank You" for all the things He gives us.

God is good, and He likes to give us good things. God wants us to ask Him for the things we need. We can ask God to give us food and clothes. We can ask God to help us get better when we are sick. We can ask God to keep us safe at night. But it's important to say "thank You" to God too. The next time you pray, remember to say "thank You" to God. —C.B.

What is something good that God has given you?

PRAYER

**Thank You, Lord, for You are good.
I will thank You as I should.**

David said to Goliath, "You are coming to fight against me with a sword. . . . But I'm coming against you in the name of the LORD who rules over all."

1 SAMUEL 17:45 NIRV

A Brave Fighter

There was a big bully named Goliath. He made fun of God's people and picked a fight with them. All of the soldiers were too scared to fight him. One day a boy named David brought food to his brothers on the battlefield. He saw how mean Goliath was. And he saw that no one stood up to Goliath. But David knew God would help him beat Goliath.

Everyone told David he couldn't win. But David trusted God. He was very brave. He said, "The Lord will save me." And guess what? God helped David beat Goliath! He was a hero to God's people.

David was brave because he knew God was with him. God is with you too. You never have to be afraid, because God is with you wherever you go. —T.M.

Who's the bravest person you know?

PRAYER

Lord, I'll be brave and will not fear because I know You're always near.

He will protect you like a bird
spreading its wings over its young.

PSALM 91:4 ICB

God Is Close

Do you know how a mother hen keeps her
baby chicks safe? When a hen feels danger
coming, she spreads out her wings. She clucks
to call her babies. All of the little chicks come
running to her. They gather under her wings.
She covers them and hides them so they are
safe.

94

The Bible tells us that God is like a bird guarding her babies. God is close to us. He is with us no matter where we are because He loves us. Even when we feel afraid, we can be sure of His love. When you are scared, God wants you to come to Him. You can do that by praying to Him. God will always be close to you. —T.M.

What color is the baby chick in the picture?

**When I feel scared I'll come to You.
Lord, You watch over all I do.**

David Becomes King

Do you remember David? He was the brave
boy who fought against Goliath. The people
liked David and wanted him to be their king.
God told David that he would be king. But
David had to wait until God said it was the
right time. The people were happy when

David became king. They poured special oil on his head to show everyone he was the new king.

Like David, we have to wait until we get older to do some things. But there are good things you can do right now. You can sing songs about Jesus. You can help your mom by picking up your toys. And when you get older, the time will be right for you to do other good things. —C.B.

What are some good things you can do today?

PRAYER

**Lord, even if I have to wait,
Your plans for me are really great.**

God is the king of the whole earth.
Make your best music for him! God rules the nations.
He sits upon his holy throne.

PSALM 47:7–8 GW

God Is Our King

Did you know that every country has a leader? During Bible times, the leaders were kings. Kings were very powerful. A king was the most important person in his country. He protected the people. He made sure they obeyed the laws. King David was the greatest king of Israel.

Some countries still have kings today. But do you know who the King of the whole world is? God is! The Bible tells us that He is the most important King of all. God is greater than all other leaders. Even David knew that God was a greater King than he was. No matter who your leader is, God is your King. You can thank Him for being the best King of all. —T.M.

How many jewels can you count in the crown?

PRAYER

**I thank You, God, that You're my King.
I lift my hands and voice to sing.**

> Sing to the LORD and give him grateful praise.
> Make music to our God on the harp.
>
> PSALM 147:7 NIRV

Make Music to God

King David was a good soldier. He was also good at music. He played the harp. He wrote many songs that praised God. You can find some of David's songs in your Bible. These songs are called psalms. In the psalms, David thanked God for being so great. He told God the things he worried about. He praised God for taking care of him. He said he was sorry when he disobeyed God.

Like King David, you can make music to God. You can sing a song to tell God you love Him. You can clap your hands or blow a horn. You can tap on a drum or shake a tambourine. God loves to hear you praise Him! —T.M.

Which instruments can you name in the picture?

PRAYER

I'll make a song of praise to You, with drums and chimes and trumpets too.

So King Xerxes put a crown on Esther's head and made her the new queen.

ESTHER 2:17 ERV

Queen Esther

The Bible tells us about a king whose name was Xerxes. One day he said, "It's time for a new queen!" He chose a young woman named Esther and put a shiny crown on her head.

Before long, Queen Esther had to make a hard choice. A bad man wanted to hurt God's people. But if Esther tried to stop him, she could be hurt! She wanted to help God's people no matter what. God kept Esther safe. And God used Esther to keep His people safe.

God has special plans for everyone who loves Him. Some people become teachers or missionaries. Some people help children who are sick. God has special plans for you too. He will help you know what they are. —C.B.

What color is the crown on Esther's head?

PRAYER

Lord, please help me understand all the things that You have planned.

> The LORD is my shepherd.
> He gives me everything I need.
>
> PSALM 23:1 NIRV

God Is Our Shepherd

A shepherd is a person who takes care of sheep. Shepherds lead their sheep where they need to go. Shepherds keep their sheep safe from other animals that might try to hurt them. They make sure the sheep have food to eat and water to drink. They watch out during the night so the sheep can rest. Sheep couldn't do much without their shepherd!

The Bible says that God is our shepherd. He goes with us wherever we go. He keeps us safe from danger. God gives us food to eat. He gives us a safe place to rest. Just like sheep need their shepherd, we need God. He will always take care of us because He loves us.
—T.M.

What sound do sheep make?

PRAYER

**Thank You, Lord, for food and rest.
Your love and care are always best.**

Let the heavens rejoice and the earth be happy!
Let the sea and everything in it shout for joy!

PSALM 96:11 ERV

Enjoy It!

God made the world a long, long time ago.
He made the sun to give us light and keep
us warm. He made pink and yellow and
purple flowers to make the world pretty. He
made birds so they could sing happy songs.
Everything God made shows us how great
and good He is. And do you know what? God
wants you to enjoy His world!

Do you like to play outdoors? Have you ever gone swimming or splashed in a pond? Maybe you like to climb a hill and run down it really fast. Maybe you like to find stones and wash them in a pail of water. Or maybe you like to see how many flowers you can count. There are many ways you can enjoy the great things God made. —C.B.

What are the kids in the picture doing?

PRAYER

Thank You, Lord, for sun and showers, swings and slides and birds and flowers.

> "My God sent his angel and shut the lions' mouths so that they couldn't hurt me."

DANIEL 6:22 GW

Hungry Lions

Lions have big teeth! Most people stay far away from lions. But did you know that a man named Daniel spent a night in a cave with lions? Daniel worked for the king. One day the king made a bad rule. He said nobody could pray to God. But Daniel loved God, so he kept praying to Him. Because Daniel did not obey the rule, he was put into a cave with lions. The king was sad because he liked Daniel. The next day the king went to the cave. He called out for Daniel. "Did God keep you safe from the lions?" Daniel said, "My God sent His angels to shut the lions' mouths." Then the king realized how great God is. He made a new rule that people should pray to Daniel's God.

Just like Daniel, you can pray to God no matter what people say. —T.M.

Can you roar like a lion?

PRAYER

**God, I know it's always right
to pray to You both day and night.**

Three times every day, [Daniel] bowed down on his knees to pray and praise God.

DANIEL 6:10 ERV

Pray Every Day

The story of Daniel shows us that it's important to pray to God. The Bible says Daniel got on his knees and prayed to God three times every day. Do you pray to God before you eat your breakfast and lunch? Do you pray before you go to bed? There are many times during the day when you can pray. You don't have to get on your knees to pray like Daniel did. But you may if you want to! You can pray when you are sitting in a chair. You can pray standing up. You can even pray when you are snuggled in your bed. When you pray, you are talking to God. He loves it when you pray, so you can pray to Him every day! —C.B.

Is the man in the picture
standing, sitting, or kneeling?

PRAYER
•

**I know You hear me when I pray.
You love to hear me every day.**

The LORD sent a big fish to swallow Jonah.
Jonah was inside the fish for three days and three nights.

JONAH 1:17 GW

Jonah and the Big Fish

God told Jonah, "Go to the city of Nineveh."
The people there were very mean. God
wanted Jonah to tell the people to obey Him.
But Jonah didn't want to go to Nineveh.
Instead, he got on a boat that went far away.
Suddenly, there was a big storm. It was so big

the sailors were afraid. Jonah knew the storm was his fault. He told the sailors to throw him into the sea!

God had put a huge fish in the sea, and it swallowed Jonah up. He stayed inside the fish for three days. He prayed to God for help and the fish spit him out. Then Jonah obeyed God and went to Nineveh.

God loves us. He wants us to obey Him. In the Bible, He tells us what He wants us to do. When we want to show God that we love Him back, He will help us obey Him. —T.M.

What kind of fish is in the picture?

PRAYER

**Help me love You as I should.
Help me do what's right and good.**

God Is Pleased

The Bible has lots of good stories. But there
are many other good things in the Bible too.
The Bible tells us that God loves us. And the
Bible tells us how God wants us to live. He
wants us to care about others. He wants us
to share and to be good helpers. He wants
us to listen to grown-ups and do our best to
obey. He wants us to say and do nice things to

everyone. When He sees people being kind to each other, He is pleased. *Pleased* is another word for happy.

Sometimes it's hard to do the right thing, but you can ask God to help you. When you show love to others, you are showing love to God. And when you love Him, He is pleased. —C.B.

What are the boys in the picture sharing?

PRAYER

Help me please You as I share Your love with people everywhere.

> "Today in the town of David a Savior has been born to you. He is the Messiah, the Lord."

LUKE 2:11 NIRV

Jesus Is Born

A manger is a food box for farm animals. But a manger was the first bed for baby Jesus!

Jesus's parents were Mary and Joseph. They went to a little town called Bethlehem. They had to be counted by the leaders of Rome. The town was crowded with other people who were being counted too. There was no room for them in the place where visitors stayed. So when Jesus was born, Mary laid Him in a manger.

An angel told the good news to some shepherds close by. "Today in the town of David a Savior has been born." Jesus was born to save us from our sins. We can be happy for His birth every day! —T.M.

What is baby Jesus lying on in the manger?

PRAYER

Thank You, Jesus, for Your birth.
Thank You that You came to earth.

> "For God loved the world so much that he gave his only Son."
>
> JOHN 3:16 ICB

So Much Love

Do you like to get presents? Do you know why people give presents? There are lots of reasons, but people often give presents to show love to someone. Presents are fun to give and they are fun to get.

The Bible tells us about the best present in the whole world. That present is Jesus! God sent Jesus from heaven because He loves us so much. Jesus is God's very own Son. God wants everyone in the world to know how much He loves them. He wants everyone to believe that Jesus is His Son.

When someone gives you a present, it's good to say "thank you." Remember to tell God "thank You" for the gift of Jesus! —C.B.

What kind of presents do you like?

PRAYER

**Thank You for Jesus who came from above.
Thank You, God, for Your gift of love.**

God's Promises Come True

There was an old man in Israel named Simeon. He loved God. God said that Simeon would not die before he saw the Savior of the world. One day God told Simeon to go to the temple. While he was there, Mary and Joseph brought in Jesus. Simeon held Jesus in his arms and praised God. He said, "I have seen with my own eyes how You will save Your people. Now all people can see Your plan." Simeon knew that God sent Jesus to be our Savior.

God's promise to Simeon came true, just like God had said. Did you know that God always keeps His promises? We can praise God like Simeon did. God is a promise keeper! —T.M.

Why was Simeon happy?

PRAYER

All of Your promises I can believe.
All of Your blessings I can receive.

Our hearts are full of joy because of him.

PSALM 33:21 NIRV

Lots of Joy

Do you know what the word *joy* means? It means that you are happy inside and out. Having joy makes you want to jump up and down or clap your hands. It makes you want to smile and sing and shout. Do you know where joy comes from? Joy comes from

knowing how much God loves you! Sometimes you have happy days, like when you can play outside with friends. But sometimes you have not-so-happy days, like when you are sick in bed. No matter what kind of day this is, you can have joy because God loves you. You can ask God to fill your heart with joy and put a smile on your face.
—C.B.

What is the girl in the picture doing?

PRAYER
●

Fill me with joy, Lord, inside and out, so I can sing and smile and shout.

Wise Men Look for Jesus

After Jesus was born a new star appeared in the sky. Some wise men from far away came to Jerusalem to look for Him. "A king has been born and we followed His star. Where is He?" they asked. The wise men found out a special king was born in Bethlehem, so they went there right away.

They followed the bright star until it stopped where Jesus was. They were happy to find Jesus! They worshipped Him and gave Him beautiful gifts.

You can worship Jesus like the wise men did. You can say, "I love You, Jesus," and sing to Him. Worshipping Jesus is like giving Him a gift. —T.M.

What color is the gift the wise man is holding in the picture?

PRAYER

**I love You, Jesus, yes I do.
I'll worship and sing a song to You.**

Good Gifts

Did you know that God likes to give us gifts? The gifts God gives to us do not come in boxes. But you can see His gifts if you look for them. The sun that shines in the sky is a gift from God. The water you drink when you're thirsty is a gift from God. Oranges that grow on trees are gifts from God too.

The Bible says that God's gifts are good and perfect. He gives us gifts because He loves us so much. The most perfect gift that God ever gave is the gift of Jesus. You can have the gift of Jesus by asking Him to come into your life. Jesus is the best gift you can get! —C.B.

What do you think
might be in the box?

PRAYER

Lord, thank You for gifts, both big and small, especially Jesus, the best gift of all.

Jesus Grows Up

The Bible tells about the day Jesus was born. Jesus is the only baby who was God's very own Son. He is the only baby who had a special star in the sky the night He was born. People came from far away to worship Him. But Jesus did not stay a baby. He grew bigger and stronger and taller just like children do.

He started walking and talking and laughing. He learned about colors and numbers and animals. Jesus kept growing and learning until He became a man. Then He told people about God's plan to save the world from sin. Jesus was a child like you are. He knows what you are thinking and feeling. You can tell Him anything and He will understand. —C.B.

What do you want to tell Jesus today?

PRAYER

**Jesus, You were once like me.
You know how growing up can be.**

Keep Growing

Do you have pictures of yourself when you were a baby? Do you look the same? No. You don't look like a baby anymore because you are growing up. When you eat food and drink water and exercise, your body grows. You even grow when you are sleeping! Your body will grow for many years until it stops.

There are other ways you can grow too. When you go to school and learn to read books, your mind will grow. The best way to grow is to learn more about God and His love for you. When you listen to Bible stories and sing songs to God, your love for Him will keep growing and growing. It never stops! —C.B.

How many books is the girl carrying in the picture?

PRAYER

Dear God, here's something that I know— my love for You will grow and grow.

Jesus Teaches Us

One day Jesus was sitting on the side of a hill.
Lots of people were listening to everything
He said. "People who are sad can be happy.
God will comfort them," He told the people.
They kept listening as He taught them more.
"Those who want to do what is right will be
happy. God will give them what they need."

Jesus also taught the people a very important rule. "Do for others what you want them to do for you."

Jesus taught the people many important things that day. And do you know what? We have His words written in the Bible. We can learn from Jesus just like all the people did on the hillside. When we read the Bible, it's like we're listening to Him. —T.M.

How does Jesus teach us today?

PRAYER

Thank You for the words You give that teach us just how we should live.

"If that is how God dresses the wild grass,
won't he dress you even better?"

MATTHEW 6:30 NIRV

God Cares for the Flowers

Did you know that everyone worries sometimes? Even grown-ups! But Jesus told us what to do when we are worried. He said, "Look how the wild flowers grow. They don't work or make clothing. But not even the richest king in fancy robes is dressed as beautifully as these flowers."

God takes care of the flowers in a field. He gives them bright sunlight and cool rain to help them grow. He makes sure they have all that they need. He watches over them all day and all night. If God cares so much about the flowers, think about how much He cares for you! —T.M.

What color is your favorite flower?

PRAYER

You dress the flowers in pink and blue. I know You'll care for my needs too.

"But not a single sparrow can fall to the ground
without your Father knowing it."

MATTHEW 10:29 NLT

God Knows Everything

Everything in the whole world belongs to
God. He takes care of the things He made.
And do you know what else is true? God
knows everything! God made so many birds
that no one could ever count them. But He
knows if one little bird falls to the ground.
He knows if a squirrel is hungry or a deer is
thirsty. He knows when a baby is born and

when a flower pops out of the ground. He knows when the sun shines and when a star shoots through the sky.

God knows all those things and He knows all about you too. He knows when you are happy or sad or tired or sick. He knows when you play and when you sleep. Do you love God? He already knows, but you can tell Him anyway! —C.B.

What color are the birds in the picture?

PRAYER

**I love that You know everything,
like when I pray or sleep or sing.**

Follow Me!

One day Jesus was walking by a big lake. He saw two brothers who were fishing. Their names were Simon and Andrew. Jesus said to them, "Come and follow me!" So they left their fishing nets and followed Jesus. Then Jesus saw two more brothers in a boat. Their names were James and John. "Follow me!" Jesus told them. So James and John got out of their boat and followed Jesus. They became Jesus's helpers.

Jesus asked other men to follow Him too. Soon He had twelve helpers. They were called disciples. They learned a lot about Jesus as they followed Him around.

You can't see Jesus today, but you can be His disciple too. Learn all about Jesus in the Bible and follow His example! —C.B.

How many disciples did Jesus have?

"Anyone who wants to serve me must follow me."

JOHN 12:26 NLT

You Can Follow Jesus

Have you ever played "Follow the Leader"? When you play this game, one person is the leader. Everyone else does what the leader does. If the leader jumps on one foot, you jump on one foot. If the leader spins in a circle, you spin in a circle too. You watch carefully and do just what the leader does.

Following Jesus is like playing "Follow the Leader." We can follow Jesus by doing the things He did. Maybe you could help someone who is sick. We can also follow Him by doing the things He told us to do. You can always be kind to others! When you do what Jesus did, you're following Him. And He's the best leader of all. —T.M.

Which boy in the picture is the leader?

PRAYER

Help me follow You each day in what I do and what I say.

The man fell to his knees and begged Jesus,
"I know that you can heal me if you will."

MARK 1:40 ICB

Jesus Makes People Better

One day a man who was sick came to Jesus. The man had bad sores on his skin. It was hard for him to walk. He knew that Jesus could make him better. "Please heal me," he said. Jesus wanted to make the man better. So Jesus touched him and said, "Be healed!" Just like that, the man's sores were gone. And he could walk again!

The Bible has many stories about Jesus making people better. One time, Jesus met a man who could not see. Jesus put mud on the man's eyes and told him to wash off the mud. When the man washed his eyes, he could see everything! Jesus also healed people who could not hear or talk.

Jesus can still make people better today. That's because He is God. —C.B.

Why is the man in the picture so happy?

PRAYER

Thank You for stories that help us know how You healed people long ago.

A happy heart is like good medicine.

PROVERBS 17:22 ICB

Good Medicine

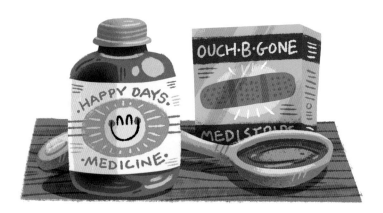

Have you ever taken medicine? Sometimes when people are sick, medicine helps them feel better. It can make stomachaches go away. It can help to stop a runny nose. When you skin your knee, medicine can help it get better faster. Medicine helps us when we don't feel our best.

The Bible says a happy heart can work like medicine. It means a happy heart makes us feel good inside. When you smile and giggle, it is good for your whole body!

The next time you feel sad, you can ask God to give you a happy heart. You can think about things that make you smile. It will be just like taking good medicine to cheer you up. —T.M.

What is one thing you can think about that makes you happy?

PRAYER

Help me have a heart that's glad even when my day is sad.

Jesus took the loaves of bread and gave thanks for them. Then he gave them to the people who were waiting to eat. He did the same with the fish.

JOHN 6:11 ERV

Dinner on the Hillside

Can you imagine making dinner for a whole town? That's what Jesus did one day. A big crowd was listening to Him teach on a hillside. After a while, they got hungry. But the people weren't able to buy food. Some of Jesus's disciples found a boy with a lunch. They brought him to Jesus and said, "He has five loaves of bread and two little fish. But that is not enough for so many people." Jesus answered, "Tell everyone to sit down." Jesus thanked God for the food the boy shared. Then He did a miracle. Jesus handed out food to the big crowd. There was enough to feed everyone! There was even some left over for the disciples.

Just like the boy, you can share what you have. Jesus can do great things when you choose to share. —T.M.

How many loaves of bread are in the picture?

Lord, even if my gifts are small,
I know that You can use them all.

And don't forget to do good and
to share what you have with others.

HEBREWS 13:16 ERV

What Can I Share?

The Bible has lots of good stories about
sharing. Do you wonder what you can share?
Here are some ideas!

If you have a brother or sister you can
share your food when you eat lunch. If a
friend comes to your house you can share
your books and toys. When your clothes get

too small, you can give them to someone else who can wear them.

You can share other things too. You can make pictures for your friends to make them smile. You can share music by singing a song for your grandma. You can share a hug with your mom or dad. And you can share a bedtime prayer with Jesus. When you share, it makes everyone happy! —C.B.

What are the children in the picture sharing?

**Help me share my books and toys
and food with other girls and boys.**

Everything Comes from God

Did you know that everything you have comes from God? From your favorite stuffed animal to the carrots on your plate, it comes from God. God has given you everything you have. He gave you the people who take care of you. He gave you the place where you live. Even the socks and shoes you put on your feet come from God!

It's good to remember that the things we have aren't really ours. They were God's first. It's easier to share when we remember that everything comes from Him. God gives you good things because He loves you. You can share some of those good things with others. When you do, you show God's love to them too. —T.M.

Can you name three things that God has given you?

PRAYER

**Thank You for the food I eat,
and for the socks that warm my feet.**

"Who is this man?" they asked each other.
"Even the wind and waves obey him!"

MARK 4:41 NLT

Jesus Calms a Storm

One day Jesus was teaching near a lake. There were many people there. So He got on a boat in the water where everyone could see Him. At night, He told His disciples, "Let's cross to the other side." They got in the boat and started across the water. Suddenly a huge storm came. Waves crashed over the side of the boat and began to fill it with water. The disciples were very afraid! But Jesus was sleeping in the back of the boat. The disciples woke Him up. They yelled, "Teacher, don't you care that we're going to drown?" Jesus got up and spoke to the waves. "Silence!" He said. "Be still!" The wind and storm stopped right away.

Jesus is in charge of everything. Even the weather obeys Him! Any time you feel afraid, you can ask Him for help like the disciples did.
—T.M.

What kind of weather do you see in the picture?

PRAYER

Jesus, You calmed the storm and sea. I know You will take care of me.

When I am afraid, I will trust you.

PSALM 56:3 ICB

Don't Be Afraid

Did you know that some people get scared when they see a big spider? Other people jump when they hear a loud noise. Sometimes you might feel afraid too. People are afraid of different things. But everyone feels afraid sometimes.

When you feel afraid, you can talk to Jesus. It's the best thing you can do! Do you remember how the disciples asked Jesus for help on the boat? You can ask Jesus for help too. Remember that Jesus always listens to you. He will help you when you ask Him. You don't have to be afraid.

No matter where you are, day or night, you can talk to Jesus. He will hear you. —T.M.

Who listens to you in the middle of the night?

**I won't be afraid; I'll bow my head.
Lord, I'll pray to You instead.**

Jesus said, "Let the little children come to me. Don't keep them away. The kingdom of heaven belongs to people like them."

Jesus and the Children

People followed Jesus wherever He went. One day some moms and dads brought their children to see Jesus. They wanted Jesus to pray for their children and bless them. Jesus's disciples thought the children would bother Jesus. They tried to send them away. But Jesus wanted to talk to the children. He wanted to show them how much He loved them. Jesus said, "Let the children come to me!" Jesus knew that children could be part of God's family too.

Jesus loves children—and that means you! You can talk to Jesus when you pray. You can listen to Jesus by reading His words in the Bible. Jesus thinks you are important. He wants you to be part of God's family. —C.B.

How many children are in the picture with Jesus?

PRAYER

Bless me, Lord, in all I do.
I'm happy You love children too.

> "You should be a light for other people. Live so that they will see the good things you do and praise your Father in heaven."

MATTHEW 5:16 ERV

Shine Your Light

Have you ever seen bright lights shining in a city at night? When it's dark you can see the lights from far away. Jesus said that you should be like a bright light shining in a city at night. When you do things to show God that you love Him, you are like a light shining in the dark.

God doesn't want us to hide His love and joy. He wants it to show in our lives! You can ask God to help you be kind to others. You can ask God to help you say nice things. You can talk about how much you love Jesus. You can share the things you are thankful for. You can help your friends pick up their toys. You can help your parents set the table. When others see the way you love God, they will praise Him too. —T.M.

How many lights do you have in your bedroom?

PRAYER

**I'll let my light shine big and bright.
I'll show Your love with all my might!**

Jesus Rides a Donkey

One day Jesus and His disciples went to a city called Jerusalem. They were there for a very special day. Jesus told two of His disciples, "Go ahead. You will find a donkey tied up and her baby with her. Untie them and bring them to me." The disciples did what Jesus said. They placed their coats on the animals' backs. Jesus sat on the baby donkey and rode into Jerusalem.

As they went down the road, many people put their coats on the ground. Others cut branches from trees and put them on the road too. It was a way of cheering for Jesus. They shouted, "Hosanna! Blessed is the one who comes in the name of the Lord!"

The people were shouting that Jesus would save them. We can shout like they did! We can praise Jesus for saving us too. —T.M.

How many legs does the donkey have?

PRAYER
•

Jesus, I'm so glad You came.
I will shout and praise Your name.

He came to the world that was his own.
But his own people did not accept him.

JOHN 1:11 ICB

The Love of Jesus

Many people loved Jesus. They believed He was the Son of God. They listened to the important words He said. They saw Jesus being kind to people. They saw Him make sick people better.

But some people did not love Jesus. Some people wanted to kill Him! The leaders thought Jesus would become a great leader.

They did not want that to happen. Their followers were mean to Jesus. They laughed at Him. They put a crown made from prickly thorns on his head. Some even hit Him and spit on Him.

Jesus knew that some people would be mean to Him. He knew they would not believe that He was God's Son. But He loved them anyway. Jesus loves everyone. He wants everyone to love Him back. —C.B.

Who does Jesus love?

PRAYER

**Jesus, You are full of love—
the Son of God, sent from above.**

The angel said . . . "Don't be afraid.
I know that you are looking for Jesus. . . .
He is not here! He has risen, just as he said he would!"

MATTHEW 28:5–6 NIRV

Jesus and the Cross

When Jesus went to Jerusalem, He knew it was time for Him to die. Soldiers put Jesus on a wooden cross to kill Him. People shouted at Him, "If You are the Son of God, come down from the cross!" But Jesus chose to die instead.

His friends were very sad. They buried Jesus in a cave. A few days later, some of them went back to the cave. Suddenly, they saw an angel! The angel said, "Jesus is not here! He is alive again! Go tell His disciples!"

Sins are all the wrong things we do. Jesus died to save us from our sins. But then He came back to life! If you ask Him to forgive your sins, He will. Whoever Jesus forgives becomes a part of His family and will live with Him forever! —T.M.

Who can forgive you for your sins?

PRAYER

Jesus, You're the only One who can forgive the things I've done.

He will make us clean from all
the wrong things we have done.

1 JOHN 1:9 ERV

Clean Again

Do you wash your hands with soap? We need to wash our hands when they get dirty. Washing our hands can make them clean again. It feels good to have clean hands.

When we do something wrong, it's called sin. Sin is like having dirt on the inside. God wants us to show our love for Him by doing what is right. He does not want us to sin.

Every day you can ask God to help you do what is right. But if you do something wrong, you can tell God you are sorry. He will forgive you and wash the sin away. It's like washing dirt off your hands.

God will forgive our sins because He loves us. God will make the sin go away and make us clean. —C.B.

Why does God forgive us?

**Forgive me, please, when I do wrong.
Your love, oh Lord, is great and strong.**

Jesus Says Good-bye

After Jesus came back to life, He went to see His disciples. Some of them couldn't believe He was really back! But as Jesus talked to them, they knew it was Him. He showed them the marks on His hands where He had been nailed to the cross.

Jesus told His disciples He had a special job for them. But they would have to wait for a special Helper. God would send the Helper after Jesus left. The Helper would be with the disciples forever!

Jesus blessed His disciples and went up to heaven. The disciples waited for the special Helper to come. Soon they would learn that God gives the Helper to everyone who is a part of His family. —T.M.

What did Jesus promise His disciples?

PRAYER

Lord, I need Your Helper too, to live a life that pleases You.

The Holy Spirit Comes

After Jesus went back to heaven, all of His disciples were in a house. Suddenly they heard the sound of wind blowing. Little flames of fire were above each person. The disciples talked in other languages! Other people did not understand what was happening. "How can these men talk in languages they do not know?" they asked.

That was the day the Holy Spirit came. The Holy Spirit was the Helper Jesus had promised! He came to people who believed in Jesus. He came to help the disciples do things they could not do before. —C.B.

Can you make the
sound of wind blowing?

PRAYER
•

**May Your Spirit give me power,
every day and every hour.**

> "I will ask the Father, and he will give you another Helper to be with you forever."
>
> JOHN 14:16 ERV

Our Special Helper

We can have the Holy Spirit just like the disciples did. When we believe that Jesus saves us from our sins, God gives us the Holy Spirit. He is our special Helper. He helps us know what is good and right. He helps us understand the Bible and remember what it says.

God sends us the Holy Spirit to help us do the things He asks us to do. The Holy Spirit helps us to obey our parents. He helps us to be kind to our friends. He also helps us know when we do something wrong so we can ask God to forgive us.

God is so good to give us a special Helper! You can thank Him for the Holy Spirit. You can ask the Holy Spirit to help you too. —T.M.

Who gives us the Holy Spirit?

PRAYER

**Holy Spirit, help me know
the way that God wants me to go.**

A Man Named Paul

Do you know what a missionary is? That's a person who tells other people about Jesus. The Bible tells us about the very first missionary. His name was Paul. After Jesus went back to heaven, Paul told many people about Him. He wanted people to know that Jesus could save them from their sins.

Sometimes Paul went far away to tell people about Jesus. Some people who didn't love Jesus put Paul in jail. But Paul kept talking about Jesus anyway. Paul even wrote letters to help other people know more about Jesus. His letters became part of the Bible. Paul loved Jesus so much that he wanted others to love Jesus too. —C.B.

Why did Paul tell people about Jesus?

PRAYER

Bless all those who go and share the truth of Jesus' love and care.

Then Jesus said to them, "So wherever you go in the
world, tell everyone the Good News."

MARK 16:15 GW

Share the Good News

When it's your birthday, do you let all
your friends know? When you learn to do
something new, do you tell people how
excited you are? When you know something
good, you want others to know too! Jesus's
love is the best thing we can know about. It's

so good He wants us to tell everyone else about it.

Jesus told His disciples that they should share the good news about His love. He told them to tell people about His love everywhere they went. You can share that good news too! When you are at the park, you can tell people about Jesus. When you are at school, you can tell people about Jesus. When you are at your neighbor's house, you can tell people about Jesus. When you do, you give people a chance to join God's family. Now that's something to get excited about! —T.M.

Who can you tell about Jesus today?

PRAYER

Jesus, there's no time to lose.
I'll tell others Your good news.

Happy Angels

The Bible tells us about angels. Sometimes God sent an angel to give someone an important message. Sometimes God sent angels to keep a person from getting hurt. The Bible says there are many angels in heaven. The angels sing praises to God. They say, "Holy, holy, holy is the Lord."

The Bible tells us something else about angels. It says they are very happy when people become Christians. Do you know how people become Christians? When people tell God they are sorry for their sins and ask Jesus to be their Savior, they become Christians. And they become part of God's big family. Any time one person in the whole world becomes a Christian, the angels are happy!
—C.B.

Who do angels sing to?

PRAYER

**The angels sing a holy song,
to praise You, Father, all day long.**

"If two or three people come together in my name, I am there with them."

MATTHEW 18:20 ICB

Meeting Together

People who believe in Jesus are called Christians. Many Christians go to church on Sunday. They go to learn more about God and sing songs to praise Him. Have you ever gone to church or Sunday school?

A long time ago, Christians didn't have churches. They would meet in houses and have dinner together. They would sing and pray and talk about God. They wanted to learn as much as they could.

Today many people meet in churches. But some Christians still meet in houses. No matter where we are, God knows when we meet together. God listens to your songs and your prayers. He talks to us through the Bible. And the Holy Spirit helps you learn more about Him. —C.B.

How can you learn more about God?

PRAYER

**God, You are my Lord and King.
You listen when I pray and sing.**

> "After I go and prepare a place for you, I will come back. Then I will take you with me, so that you can be where I am."
>
> JOHN 14:3 ERV

Jesus Is Coming Back

We have learned many great things about Jesus. The Bible tells us that He made the whole world. The Bible says He loved and helped the people around Him. The Bible tells us that Jesus died on a cross for our sins. Wouldn't it be nice to meet Jesus face-to-face?

Before He went back to heaven, Jesus told His friends that He would come back to earth someday. We don't know when that day will be. But we know it will happen, because everything Jesus says is true.

When Jesus comes back, everyone who believes in Him can go to heaven with Him. Heaven is a very special place. It is always light in heaven. It is always happy in heaven. The Bible says that heaven is more beautiful than anywhere else. If you believe in Jesus, you can be with Him in heaven forever! —C.B.

How do we know Jesus will come back someday?

PRAYER

Lord, I believe in what You say— that You are coming back someday.

About the Authors

Crystal Bowman is a best-selling, award-winning author of more than one hundred books for children including *The One Year Book of Devotions for Preschoolers, My Grandma and Me,* and *J Is for Jesus.* She also writes lyrics for children's piano music and stories for *Clubhouse Jr.* magazine. She is a mentor and speaker for MOPS (Mothers of Preschoolers) and teaches workshops at writers' conferences. She enjoys writing books for kids of all ages and wants them to know that God loves them and cares about them very much. Crystal is a mother and grandmother. She and her husband live in Florida where she likes to walk on the beach.

Teri McKinley grew up in the world of publishing, attending book signings and book conventions with her mother, Crystal Bowman. She began writing stories in elementary school and her love for writing grew in college. In addition to writing greeting cards for Discovery House, Teri has co-authored several books including *Our Daily Bread for Kids, M Is for Manger,* and *My Mama and Me.* Teri and her husband live in Texas and serve in several ministries at their church. Above all, Teri's favorite job is being a mom to their son.

Illustrator **Luke Flowers** spent countless childhood hours drawing sports heroes and comics at his grandfather's drawing desk. His love of art led him to Rocky Mountain College of Art and Design, where he earned a BFA in illustration. After ten years working for Young Life in the Creative Services Department, he launched Luke Flowers Creative, a company that seeks to "bring the illumination of imagination" to every project. Luke has won fourteen gold and silver Addy Awards for illustration and design.

ONE BIG STORY

Several fun ways to learn it!

Short and engaging children's devotions,
easy-to-remember Bible verses, exciting facts,
and fun illustrations make the ***Our Daily Bread for Kids***
devotional an excellent way to teach
your children ages 6–10 more about God.

Help us get the word out!

Our Daily Bread Publishing exists to feed the soul with the Word of God.

If you appreciated this book, please let others know.

- Pick up another copy to give as a gift.
- Share a link to the book or mention it on social media.
- Write a review on your blog, on a bookseller's website, or at our own site (ourdailybreadpublishing.org).
- Recommend this book for your church, book club, or small group.

Connect with us:

 @ourdailybread

 @ourdailybread

 @ourdailybread

Our Daily Bread Publishing
PO Box 3566
Grand Rapids, Michigan 49501 USA

 books@odb.org